D1722885

The Sassy Way to

RANKING #1
IN GOOGLE
WITH
SEO

when you have NO CLUE…

by Gundi Gabrielle

*This is a **SassyZenGirl** Guide*

TABLE OF CONTENTS

The Art of Ranking in Google

Have you ever wondered how websites end up on page 1 in Google - and…. why your site isn't there?

Does it just "happen"?

Is it luck?

Do you need to know someone at Google?

Or…… are there actual techniques that can help you get to #1?

The good news is: there *are*!

The Art of Ranking in Google is called SEO and people who do it well, make a LOT of money!

Why?

Because the higher you rank, the more people will visit your site = potential customers -> the more money you can make.

SEO is a form of internet marketing, just like Google or Facebook Ads, yet a lot more effective and stable once set up - and in the long run, far less expensive!

For blogging purposes, SEO is next to Kindle Publishing *the* most effective strategy to grow an audience long term - and also, to market affiliate products (=monetize your site).

And you need to start from Day 1. - This is the one technique you can*not* put off for later!

Why?

Because it takes time to build authority with Google and - even more importantly - understanding SEO will affect your entire site structure and how you write your posts!

If you don't learn it now, all your posts might have to be rewritten later - or they won't rank. So, even if you feel a little overwhelmed by all this new information, try to hang on a little longer - and you will be glad you did.

I'll try to make it as painless as possible....;-)

SEO can be fun once you understand how it works - and especially once you start seeing result!

So give it some time, apply consistent action and enjoy the process!

All very the best &
Happy Blogging!

Gundi Gabrielle
SassyZenGirl.com

Chapter 1 - What is SEO...?

SEO stands for "Search Engine Optimization".

What are Search Engines?

Google, Bing and Yahoo are the three best known search engines, but most SEO efforts focus on Google since that is by far the most widely used.

In a nutshell - SEO is the art of ranking on page 1 in Google - ideally the #1 spot.

Why would that be important?

Because the higher you rank the more organic traffic (=people googling) your site will receive and with that potential new readers and customers.

To understand how powerful SEO is, lets look at a few numbers:

Statistics show that page 1 in Google gets 95% of all search traffic (=people googling)!

Page 2 receives 5%. Page 3 only 1%.

Let that sink in for a moment....

Even more staggering - 61% of traffic go to the #1-3 spots.

The #1 spot actually gets a staggering 33-40% of all search traffic on Google!!

That is HUGE!

In comparison, only 10% go to paid Ads - even though ads are very expensive, whereas organic ranking is mostly free (once you get there....).

That's why SEOs are some of the highest paid marketing consultants in the world with up to 20K per month per client!

Yes, you heard correctly!

The monthly revenue from having a site rank #1 in a competitive niche will be a LOT higher than those 20K, which is why companies are more than happy to pay well.

I have several friends - my SEO mentors in fact - who make 100,000 Dollars **per month** from SEO!

It sounds incredible, but these are not singular cases, but remarkably frequent.

This income comes from both:

* **SEO clients** = companies who want to rank their websites in the top spots. Note that SEO Consulting is always a monthly service because it takes consistent effort to get to the top spots and stay there

- and -

* **Affiliate sites** - your own sites where you market affiliate products for a commission. Obviously, that, too, requires a high degree of SEO expertise, otherwise, you'll have to pay for Google and

Facebook ads - and still won't have remotely the same results

How does SEO work?

Google's #1 concern is to provide the most relevant high quality content to whatever phrase (= "Keyword") someone puts into the search bar when "googling".

SEO therefore is about you convincing Google that your content is the best and most relevant available for this search term.

That's what it's all about.

How do you convince Google?

Well, first of all, you are not convincing a person/ an employee at Google. That would be absurd and physically impossible given the billions of searches every day.

Instead, Google employs little cyber "bots" that constantly crawl the net and every page on there. The bots catalogue all your content and determine what it is about and how valuable/relevant it is.

So you need to send signals that the Google bots can understand - and do so consistently.

You need to build up "authority" with Google. Prove that you are a reputable site with quality content that will be truly helpful to their readers.

Obviously, that takes time, especially when your site is brand new, but you can greatly speed up the process by employing a number of SEO techniques.

That's what this book will teach you.

Keywords vs. Niches

To clarify - you don't just "rank", you always rank for a specific search term or "keyword" as they are called. For example, someone might google:

How do I potty train my Dog?

If you want to rank on page 1 for that keyword, you will need to SEO "optimize" your article for that phrase.

In other words, your site will rank for many different search terms - each on a different rank within the "SERPs" = the result pages that come up after you google something.

SERPs = "Search Engine Result Pages"

And it's not just individual posts. If "dog training" is your main niche, then your entire site needs to be optimized for that keyword.

Optimization happens both "On Page"= on your site and "Off Page" = anything that points or links to your site.

The more competitive a keyword, e.g. the more people are trying to rank for it, the more difficult it will be to reach the top spots. In some cases, it will be impossible for you with a brand new site.

This is where "Authority "comes in.

Sites like *Wikipedia, CNN, National Geographic* etc. enjoy huge authority with Google, because they are long established and highly regarded.

You cannot "beat" those sites in the beginning and there are also certain keywords/search phrases that you simply will not be able to rank for in the first year or two, such as:

"Make money online"
"Weight Loss"
"Lawyer New York"

Those are highly competitive keywords with millions of sites trying to rank for them.

Notice, I say "keywords" - not "niches". Because even in very competitive niches, you can still rank and monetize your site - but for a *different type* of keyword…. more on that in Chapter 2.

White Hat vs. Black Hat SEO

There are a number of SEO techniques that can greatly speed up the process, and they are grouped into "White Hat" and "Black Hat" techniques.

As you probably guessed *White Hat* follows Google's rules and policies, but is by far not as fast and effective, while *Black Hat* techniques can help you rank very quickly, but come with a significant risk of getting penalized or de-indexed (= your site being banned from Google - and you don't ever want that to happen!)

In this book, we will only cover *White Hat* techniques as those will give you plenty to start with - and without running into trouble with Google.

How does Google determine where to rank you?

Google doesn't exactly tell us - that's the whole point - and their ranking algorithm keeps changing to adjust to ever new *Black Hat* tactics.

You may have heard of "Panda" and "Penguin" updates and wondered what that was all about?
We'll cover those in the last chapter, but for now let me just say:

SEO is a constant game of hide and seek between Google changing its algorithm and SEOs then trying to figure out how to rank within that new algorithm.

Once they find effective ways, Google responds with another update and a stricter set of rules to keep it fair and punish unethical techniques. And then we start again....

It's important to understand that unless a page has huge authority like *CNN, Forbes, Wikipedia,* or *Amazon,* any site ranking on page 1 for very competitive terms is applying at least a few Black Hat techniques.

It's impossible to get there otherwise, unless you give it years and years to grow authority naturally.

That's ok as long as that site is providing value and helpful content. Gone are the days where SEOs could just spam the heck out of a site and rank #1. These days, they would quickly be slapped with a penalty and de-indexed (=disappear from Google).

As I mentioned before, Google's #1 priority is to provide the best, most relevant content to their customers that's available *right now.*

SEO therefore is about sending the "right" signals to the Google bots to get ranked as high as possible. The bots are not people, they don't think or feel, instead they are programmed to respond to certain signals and then rank that site accordingly.

What signals are the Google bots looking for?

Most of all, **authority** and **relevance**.

You need to show that you are an expert and that your content is the most relevant - while you are competing with every other related site on the internet!

Scary?

Not really….;-) - if you understand a few basic principles and techniques - and have some patience!

Building authority with Google takes time, especially with a brand new site. You have to prove that you are worthy of the exposure and the newer the site, the more skeptical Google will be - understandably.

So start as soon as your site is set up and apply the principles taught here consistently. Over time, you will see results, and once Google starts taking you seriously, it becomes more of a self runner.

Maintaining your status will be much easier than getting there, so your initial effort is well worth it in the long run.

Keep in mind also that the majority of bloggers never bother to learn these principles. And unless you are in a very competitive niche with lots of knowledgable people, it won't take that much effort to get to page 1. But it takes *consistent* effort - and excellent keyword research.

During the initial months, while you are building trust with google, you can use other techniques like Social Media Marketing, Kindle books, and the techniques taught in book #2 of this series to drive "traffic" (=potential readers) to your side.

Eventually you will be able to rely more and more on SEO and no longer have to hustle, network and pay for ads. You can still continue with those, but on a much smaller scale, because in the long run, SEO is the most effective - and consistent - traffic generator on the internet!

What parameters does Google look at?

Google looks at 3 areas:

* On Page

* Off Page

* Social Media

On Page is everything that happens on your website. How you structure your site. How you interlink your pages, how you write your posts etc.

Is there a clear site structure that the bot can easily read?

Do you add fresh, quality content on a regular basis?

Is that content optimized for the keywords you are trying to rank for?

Is there a lot of interaction with your readers in the form of comments, social media shares etc.?

Off Page is everything pointing at your site = Backlinks from other sites, incl. social media. You might have heard the term "Link Juice". That's what this is referring to:

How many sites are linking to you? and most importantly, are they of high quality/authority or are they spammy sites?

As an example, the *New York Times* linking to one of your articles will greatly boost your authority, whereas low quality backlinks from spammy sites can seriously harm you.

If your friend links to you from a brand new website, it will also not have much weight, no matter how nice or proficient your friend is. His/her "Domain Authority" will be zero and that's exactly how much link juice you get - zero. Still good to interlink, because those sites will grow and you can both boost each other's authority over time.

We will cover Off Page more in Chapter 3.

Social Signals are a more recent addition to Google's ranking algorithm, but have since greatly gained in importance. A site without any social signals - likes, shares, retweets etc - will not rank, and that makes sense.

In this day and age, any relevant, helpful or inspiring article will be shared on social media, so if there are no social signals, but a lot of backlinks, something is clearly not right and Google will respond accordingly.

A scenario like the above would look fishy and is often a sign of Black Hat techniques, because, yes, you can manufacture backlinks to boost your authority, and Google is always on the lookout for any suspicious behavior.

You will need to address all 3 areas, and all of them together determine how Google will rank you.

One more thing….

It's important to understand, that Google ranks your urls, in other words your domain name/web address (YourAwesomeSite.com) - ***not*** your content.

Whatever you accomplish stays with that domain name. If you change it, you have to start all over again, even if you transfer all your articles to the new domain!

Yet another important reason not to waste time on commercial blogging platforms like *Blogger*, *Weebly* or

WordpressCOM (not be confused with the non-profit, free *WordpressORG* software that most bloggers use):

When you leave these very limiting platforms - and you will eventually if you are serious about blogging and making money online - you might loose your domain name and then all the work and effort you put in over weeks and months will be lost and you have to start all over again.

Therefore, if you haven't already, find a good web hosting company and get your site self hosted.

The link below will give you a whopping **50% discount** for one of the **top rated Web Hosting** Services in the business:

SassyZenGirl.com/Web-Hosting

Or do your own research and find a suitable service.

But start now - don't put it off. It will be much more work a few months down the road and you might even have to hire someone to transfer your site.

<u>Please note:</u> in the print version of this book, all links are presented as "Pretty Links", meaning they all have the url

SasyZenGirl.com + a short ending for each link to make it easy for you to enter them into the search bar.

Pretty Link is a Wordpress plugin that redirects complicated lengthy urls via a short "pretty" link.
= easy to ready / easy to copy+paste

Chapter 2 - On Page SEO

First things first....

Before we get into optimizing your site and blog posts, we need to make sure the following two elements are in place and properly set up:

* *Mobile Compatibility* (= how well does your site design adjust and function to mobile devices?)

* *Site Speed* (= how quickly does your site load?)

Mobile-Friendly

In one of the more recent algorithm updates (April 2015), Google made it a requirement for every site to be "mobile friendly".

A lot of web sites lost their ranking, because they didn't pay attention or didn't update in time, so be sure to take care of this right from the start.

A staggering 70% of users access the internet through mobile devices these days, so it is really important that your site looks good and is fully functional on all.

Fortunately, most themes are now "mobile friendly", so you shouldn't run into any problems, but always make sure "responsive" is listed as a feature whenever you review a Wordpress theme.

To test your site you can use *Googles's Mobile-Friendly Test:*

Search.Google.com/Search-Console/Mobile-Friendly

Site Speed

You have probably visited sites that take forever to load. It's really frustrating and I usually just press the back button and find a faster alternative.

Google is aware of this behavior and punishes slow sites. You will not ever rank high with a slow loading site.

An easy way to test your site's speed is Google Page Speed Insights:

Developers.Google.com/Speed/PageSpeed/Insights/

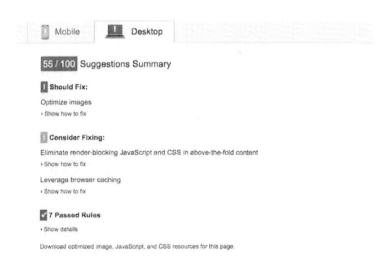

You can enter your site name and will get two speed metrics - one for mobile devices and one for desktop.

Ideally, both values should be green. Occasionally, yellow is still ok, but the numbers should not be lower than 70, ideally above 80.

If your site does not meet those requirements, Google will provide you with a number of instructions on how to improve site speed. It's a rather complex and time consuming task, so I usually outsource to someone on **Fiverr** or **Konker**.

This is one of the gigs I have used in the past, pretty inexpensive, and I can focus my time on other things:

SassyZenGirl.com/Site-Speed-Gig

Plugins that improve Site Speed

There are number of free Wordpress plugins that will greatly help with site speed. I would recommend installing at least the first 3:

1) **Database Optimizer**: *WPOptimize*

By default, WordPress stores every post, page, and comment including post revisions, trash data, and information from various plugins.

WP Optimize helps you de-clutter your database by removing stale post revisions, spam comments, trashed items, and removal of transient options.

Less clutter = more speed!

2) Caching Plugin: *W3 Total Cache or WP Super Cache*

A caching plugin stores your site's images, files and data on the server, so it doesn't have to load the website from scratch every time someone visits. Instead, the static version of your site is displayed. This saves a lot of resources and works with any type of website.

3) Photo Optimizer: *WPSmush.it*

High quality photos can greatly slow down a site's loading speed. As a general rule, always save your photos at no more than 100KB total size and at the actual dimensions that the photos will show in the post. *Photoshop, Apple Preview* and various other photo softwares allow you to set those parameters without loosing quality.

A plugin like *WP Smush.it* will further ensure that images are properly compressed and use appropriate formats.

This plugin reduces image file sizes, improves performance, strips the metadata from JPEGs, and removes unused colors from indexed images.

4) **Lazyloader:** *BJ Lazy Load*
Allows you to "lazy load" post images and thumbnails by replacing them with a placeholder. The images are only loaded as they are about to become visible in a user's browser.

5) *P3 Profiler*
If you notice problems with site speed, this plugin can help identify if any of your installed plugins are responsible.

To install any of the above plugins, open your WP Admin Board, go to Plugins -> Add New -> enter the plugin name in the search bar, click "install" -> "activate".

On Page Optimization

On Page Optimization should start from the time you first set up your blog or website.

Really…..don't wait with this!

It will take a lot longer to correct everything later, especially once your site is growing and there are many pages and sub pages. Get it right from the start and then keep applying with every new page and post you add.

No SEO technique will work without proper On Page Optimization - so this is where you need to start.

What is On Page Optimization?

The art of making your site and posts easily readable for the Google bots. Sending the "right" signals, so your site appears relevant and offering great information.

These are the 3 areas you need to cover:

* Keyword Research

* Optimize your overall site structure

* Optimize each page and post

Lets start with keywords. This is where the money is!

Unless you learn keyword research well, ranking will be very difficult, no matter what techniques you use, so let's dig right in....

Keyword Research

What are "Keywords"?

Keywords are the words and phrases we put in Google's search bar when we try to find something - e.g. when we "google".

In other words, a keyword is usually not just one word, but a phrase like "how to bake Christmas cookies" or "latest movie releases".

Phrases like that are called "Long Tail Keywords", consisting of anywhere between 3-10 words, and those LT keywords are the ones you want to rank for initially.

Why not rank for Short Tail Keywords?

Good question! - Why would you not want to rank for 1-2 word phrases like "loosing weight", "budget travel" or "parenting advice"?

Because short tail keywords are extremely competitive - at least most of them.

Page 1 in Google is usually filled with high authority sites like *Wikipedia, Forbes, CNN, Amazon* or whichever sites are the top authorities in that particular field.

It would be impossible for you to compete with them or rank anywhere near page 1 for highly competitive, more general terms.

Instead we want to focus on Long Tail Keywords with a decent **search volume** (at least 100 per month) and not too much **competition**, meaning not too many other sites are trying to rank for the same term.

From now on - each of your posts will focus on one main Long Tail Keyword and you can sprinkle a few related or synonymous keywords throughout. Those are also called "LSI" keywords = latent semantic indexing (no need to remember that phrase…;-).

For the reader, this will not be noticeable, in case you are concerned. Keyword density should be around 1%, so just enough to signal the Google bots what they should rank you for without being annoying to the reader.

How do we find rankable LT Keywords?

Keyword Research consists of analyzing **search volume** and **competition**. Don't worry, it's easier than you think…;-)

* Analyze Search Volume

Lets start with Google! - We enter a keyword idea

(blog post topic) into the search bar - in this example "Building a Tree House".

When I enter this phrase you notice that Google immediately shows me related keywords that are frequently searched for:

This is helpful to get more ideas. You can find even more options when you scroll to the bottom:

Play around with those phrases and see what other LT Keywords Google shows you and then write down the ones that could apply to your post idea.

You can also add "Best", "Top", "Easiest", "Cheapest" or whatever specification applies to your topic. This will narrow it down even further and offer more options.

Next, we visit the **Google Keyword Planner (GKP)** to find out how many monthly searches a keyword receives = how many times per month someone types in that specific keyword into Google's search bar.

If you completed **Book #2** in this series, you will already have used **GKP**, if not, here is how you set it up:

First, you need to create a *Google Adwords* account. Don't worry, you don't have to run ads or spend money. It's only to get access to the keyword planner tool.

Go to **Adwords.Google.com/ko/KeywordPlanner/** and follow the prompts.

Once your account is set up, you can start your research.

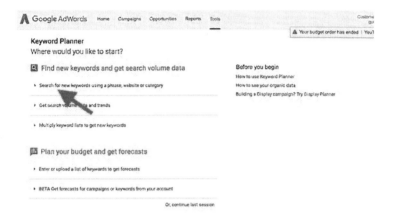

Enter a niche or search term - I used "Treehouse" in this example.

You have a few options to customize your search, including specific locations if you offer a local service or product, filters, negative keywords etc.

Then scroll down and click "Get ideas" to open this window with the monthly search results:

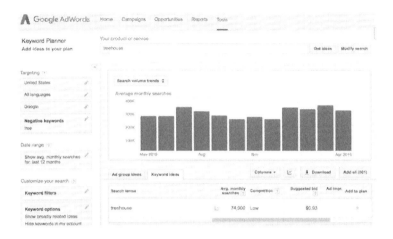

Please note that Google no longer gives out exact amounts unless you start an ad campaign, however, just the range is sufficient here.

For your main long tail keyword you want ideally at least 500 searches per month, more is better - at a very minimum 100.

The keyword "treehouse" has 74,000 searches which is a lot, but I also used a short tail term here - more the general niche than a specific phrase to see what Long Tail phrases the Keyword planner would suggest to me.

For this, we scroll down and can now view related terms and their search volume. A great way to get Long Tail keyword ideas and see right away whether they have enough search volume to be viable candidates.

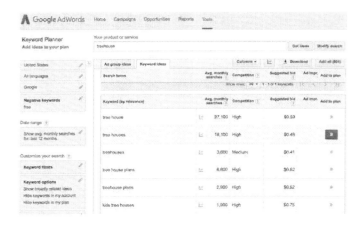

Notice how "treehouse" "tree house" "tree houses" and "treehouses" all have entirely different search volumes - huge differences actually. So those little details are very, very important. These are 4 entirely different keywords as far as the Google bots are concerned.

Don't pay attention to the "competition" value. That's related to ad campaigns and affiliate products and has nothing to do with "your" SEO competition.

Another free tool to give you a wide range of related keyword ideas is **UberSuggest.org**.

Simply enter a keyword idea or genre and you will receive an extensive list of possible combinations.

* Analyzing the Competition

To find out how **competitive** a keyword is, we start by entering the phrase into the Google search bar and see what pages show on page 1, in particular the first 5 spots.

If you see a lot of well known = high authority sites like *wikipedia*, major media outlets, publishers, blogs etc., then the keyword is probably too competitive. You will not get to page 1 anytime soon, let alone the top 3, and unless you rank there, traffic from Google will be minimal.

If, however, you see mostly unknown sites, it's worth researching further. For this, you need to install the **MOZ Toolbar**, a browser extension. It's free and will show you immediately how authoritative the other sites are.

Authority & Trust

Before we install MOZ, let me clarify the two most relevant metrics that are used to define site authority and trust in the eyes of Google.

1) **Domain Authority (DA)** & Page Authority (PA) - assigned by **MOZ.com**

2) **Trust Flow (TF)** & Citation Flow (CF) - assigned by **Majestic.com**

It's important to understand that neither metric is officially assigned by Google! Both are simply approximations used to assist in SEO research and based on Google ranking behavior as it is currently being observed.

Google used to assign "Page Rank", but has since abandoned that metric and not updated the numbers in years. Therefore, Page Rank is now considered irrelevant (in case you ever come across that term).

None of the above metrics are infallible, but in most cases give a pretty accurate description of how much authority and trust a site enjoys with Google. A good basis, but not perfect, plus it usually takes a few weeks before changes are reflected in the score.

MOZ Tool Bar gives you access to DA and PA as well as the number of backlinks to a side (see the black bar underneath each listing). We will discuss backlinks and how to read them in the **3ʳᵈ chapter**, for now lets look at DA and PA.

Domain Authority refers to the entire site, whereas Page Authority refers to a particular page/article on that site. Most important for our research will be DA, the overall authority of a site.

In case you are wondering - a domain is the name of your website, the URL as it's also called:

YourAwesomeWebsite.com

You can also check DA and PA at:

Moz.com/ResearchTools/ose/

If most sites on page 1 have a DA below 20, you have a good chance of ranking there. If the site has less then 10 backlinks, even more so.

Often however, keywords with low competition also have very low search volume. So while you could rank easily, it wouldn't help much, because not too many people are looking for that phrase.

The key here - and this can take a little bit of time - is to find keywords with little to no competition that still have at the very least 100 monthly searchers, ideally more.

The other main metric is *Trust Flow* which you can check on **Majestic.com**. You get 2 free searches per day, and the result will look something like this:

Once again, if sites have a TF of mostly <20, you have a good chance of ranking. If most are over 30, move on.

This is not an exact science, nor are these exact numbers to go by - by no means! - Ranking depends on many different factors and you will get a better feeling for what works over time.

The above ranges are good estimates to go by when you first start - to have at least a basic idea of what is realistic and what is not.

Here are more factors to look at when determining competitiveness of a keyword:

Are competitor listings keyword optimized?

In addition to DA, TF and number of backlinks, also check the following in your competitors' SERP listings:

- do they use the *exact* keyword phrase in the headline? And if so, how far in the front?

- do they use the keyword in the url?

- do they use it in the meta description (the short text underneath the title)

If not - it will be much easier to outrank them, even if they have a higher authority score than you. That's why Long Tail keywords are so powerful, because if you are the only one optimizing for that specific phrase, there is a good chance that Google will rank you higher, even if you are new and don't have much authority yet!

Read that last sentence a few times to let it sink in, because that - at the core - is the art of effective keyword research.

Again, no *one* metric will ever give you a definite prediction - and even when everything seems right, Google doesn't always respond or takes time, sometimes months.

But the more of these factors are in place, the more *likely* it is that you can rank on page 1 - or ideally #1 - for that particular keyword phrase.

In the beginning, and especially if you don't have a lot of time, it is helpful to use keyword research tools to do the heavy lifting for you.

The most effective and still reasonably priced is **Long Tail Pro**. You can simply enter your keyword idea and the program will provide you with a long list of possible Long Tail Options together with a score for competitiveness. You can access it here:

SassyZenGirl.com/Keyword-Research-Tool

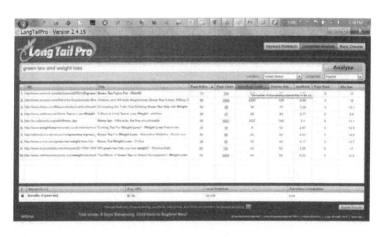

If this is still too expensive, I can recommend this Konker gig, for just $10 per niche:

SassyZenGirl.com/Keyword-Gig

It will be money well spent - and saves a LOT of time doing the research yourself.

Do you need to do keyword research for every single article?

Not necessarily, but definitely for every article you want to rank for.

So if you have a regular schedule of, lets say, 1 post per week, then at a minimum have at least 1 post per month with a more in-depth article and thorough keyword research - and also build some backlinks to that post (see **Chapter 3**).

That way it doesn't become too overwhelming or expensive in the beginning, but you are still beginning to build authority and over time will see results in the form of higher rankings.

Steady does it with SEO and that would be a good basic schedule.

Now lets see how we can employ keywords on your site and specific posts…

Optimizing your Site

Optimization of your site covers a number of different areas:

Your Site's Meta Data

Meta data include your site's name/title, tag line/sub title and snippet (the short description that shows in google).

It is helpful for SEO purposes to include keywords relating to your niche in the meta data - and your url (= site name).

The purpose here is to tell Google as often as possible - without spamming - what your site is about.

Having a keyword in your domain name, can also help with ranking - either:

the **full domain = EMD = exact match domain** - *Example: DogTraining.com* or **partial domain = PMD = partial match domain** - *Example: OnlineDogTraining.com*

These days, PMDs are safer since Google is toughening "Over-Optimization" rules. That's when you stuff your keyword everywhere. Google considers that spamming and will downgrade or even penalize your site.

EMDs are easier to rank, BUT you have to know exactly how often and where you can use the main keyword and that takes time to learn. PMDs also rank well, and you still have to watch keyword placement, but it's less contentious, so I would go with that (or no match) in the beginning.

For local businesses, also include your location, for example: *PlumberDallasTX.com* - or similar. Makes it much easier to rank in a local market.

You can enter all your meta data here:

Settings -> General Settings -> enter your site name and tag line

Also be sure to indicate here whether you want to use:
http:// - or - **http://www.**

for "WP Address" and "Site Address".

To Google those are two completely separate domains with two different scores for Trust Flow.

Pick *one* version, enter it here and use it consistently whenever you share your url or build links.

When you check Trust Flow in Majestic, always check both "root domain" (bare url) & "sub domain" (with www.) in the search bar. Whichever has the higher score, is the *main* Site Address - the one that all SEO efforts are directed to - and the only one you should consider in your research.

Permalink Structure

Next, lets set up an SEO friendly Permalink structure. That's how your post url appears, see below.

Within your WP Admin Board, go to *"Settings"* -> *Permalinks* and check the option with the red arrow: Even without SEO, that url structure is much more pleasant on the eye - and much easier to read for the

google bots. This is where you will always place your main keyword.

Interlinking

It is VERY important to interlink your pages and especially *related* blog posts. This again, helps the Google bots understand how your site is structured and how everything is connected. We will go into more detail when we **optimize your first post**, but for now make sure your home page links to all other top level pages (About, Blog, Contact, Services etc.).

Linking does not mean - linking through the "Menu". You need to create a link on the home page to each of the other sites. The link text can be anything. It doesn't have to say "here is my About page" or similar. Just link from the home page to each main sub page and then from those to any further sub pages.

Whenever you write a post, be sure to link to at least 2-3 (related) posts and vice versa. Once again, it helps the Google bots understand what articles are related and/or form a sub group on your site.

In the beginning when you only have a few pages, this may not seem very important, but once your site grows to a few hundred - it will become *very* important, especially over years…

Yoast SEO Plugin

Before we go into the details of On Page optimization, lets first install a very important tool - ***Yoast SEO*** plugin.

It's free, the #1 rated SEO plugin around, and you can download and activate it from within your Wordpress admin board.

*Go to "Plugins" (left side bar in WP admin board) -> Add New -> enter **Yoast SEO** in the search bar -> Install -> Activate*

You will see the "SEO" tab in the left side bar. This is where you will customize the plugin.

For the most part, you can use the defaults, but two things need to be set up manually:

1) Connect with Google Search Console

2) Generate Sitemaps

Google Search Console

It's important to connect your new site with the *Google Search Console (GSC)*.

Any communication with Google about your site will happen through your GSC account. You can also access many other helpful features and stats. To see them all, just watch a *Google Search Console* Tutorial in Youtube.

This article by Yoast will show you how to set up your *GSC* account and connect with the *Yoast SEO* plugin.

It's very easy. Will only take 5 minutes, so best do it now and have that out of the way.

SassyZenGirl.com/Yoast-GSC

Installing a Sitemap

Next, you want to upload a Sitemap to make it easier for the Google bots to crawl and rank your site.

Yoast SEO can create sitemaps for you - _after_ you connected the plugin to your GSC (see **prior chapter**). This is how you do it:

1. On your Search Console home page, select your website.

2. In the left sidebar, click **Crawl** and then **Sitemaps**.

3. Remove outdated or invalid sitemaps like **sitemap.xml**

4. Click the **Add/Test Sitemap** button in the top right.

5. Enter **sitemap_index.xml** into the text box that appears.

6. Click **Submit**.

Done!

Google Analytics

*NOTE: if you read the first book in the blogging series and already set up your Google Analytics account, you can **skip this chapter and go to Optimizing Your Posts**.*

❖ ❖ ❖ ❖ ❖ ❖ ❖ ❖ ❖ ❖ ❖ ❖

The most important tool for analyzing and tracking your blog traffic will be *Google Analytics*. It is the industry standard for website analytics and an absolute must.

Google Analytics helps you to assess how well pages, posts and features are doing, who your audience is and where your traffic is coming from.

If you ever want to work with advertisers, PR agencies or sponsors, they will want statistics pulled from *Google Analytics*, so it is important to get it set up from the start.

Even if you are not planning to monetize your site, it will still be an important tool to help you measure what works and what doesn't, and how to grow your audience.

Once again, Youtube has plenty of Tutorials showing you all the different features Google Analytics has to offer. For now, lets focus on setting it up and connecting it with your site.

Setting Up Google Analytics

Go to ***analytics.google.com*** and sign up by following the prompts. If you don't have a Google account yet (e.g., through a gmail address) you will be asked to create one, but you can use your regular email address (doesn't have to be gmail).

Next, you will be guided to this screen for ***Google Analytics*** **sign up**:

Click **Sign up** and on the next screen follow the prompts:

Account: This will be the "umbrella name" for your GA account. You can have several different websites under one account, but this is the overall name. You can use your blog's name or any other name.

Property: Enter your website name and url.

Scroll down and click, **Get tracking ID**.

Next, you will see some code - no need to panic…;-) - just hang in there…

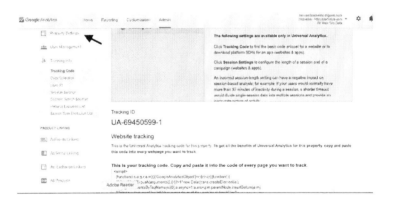

First, go to

Admin -> **Property Settings** -> turn on each of the tabs under **Advertising Features**. This will give you additional data from each visitor. These need to be turned on from the start to deliver accurate data.

Now back to the code. Thankfully, there is a great plugin that will place the code for you, making things very easy:

Google Analyticator

If you haven't already installed and activated this plugin, do it now, and then click on the **Google Analytics** tab in the left *WordPress* Admin bar.

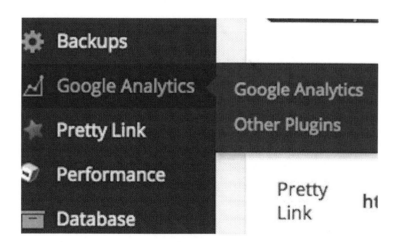

This will lead you to **Basic Settings**. Make sure that **Google Analytics logging** is **enabled**, and select the correct **Analytics Account**. Then press **Save**.

Next, you will see a message in your dashboard: *"Don't miss your crawl errors: connect with Google Search Console here."*

Click on the link, then click on **Get Google Authorization Code**.

In the pop-up, click **Allow**, and then copy and paste the prompted code into the box. Then click **Authenticate** and **Save Profile**.

All done!

Seeing Your First Statistics

Google updates data several times a day. Go to **Reporting** and try the various options in the left hand sidebar. To see who is on your site right now, click **Real time -> Overview**.

Of course, you won't see anything right after set-up, so give it a day, or at least a few hours, and then check again.

Optimizing your Posts

Now you are ready to optimize your posts and pages. You can also follow along via this video:

SassyZenGirl.com/Onpage-SEO

Where to place your Keyword?

Headline

Your keyword has to be part of your headline, ideally in the beginning or as far in the front as possible. Also watch this when you analyze your competition. Do they have the exact keyword phrase in the headline and if so where? If they don't, it will be much easier to outrank them.

URL

Make the url the main keyword. This is very important and will go a long way in helping you to rank. Also, watch this when analyzing the competition.

First Paragraph

Mention the main keyword once in the first paragraph to establish what the post is about (for the Google bots)

1% Keyword Density

Mention keyword approx. once per 100 words. Doesn't have to be exact, but as a general guideline. More can be considered "keyword stuffing" (spam in Google's eyes...), less is too vague a signal for the Google bots .

Yoast SEO will tell you the keyword density of your posts, so it's very easy to check (see below).

H2 (=largest Sub Heads -> "Heading 2")

Mention the main keyword once in an H2. Again - once only - not in every H2!

This is where you set up H2s (biggest sub head option):

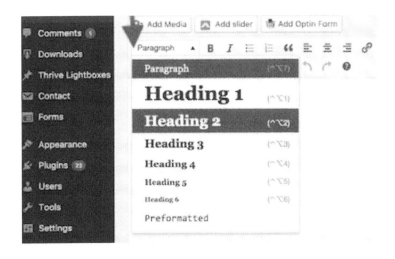

Highlight the text you want to turn into a "Heading" and then click the above.

Picture Alt text

Always have at least 1 picture per article. More is better. Google loves visual media!

Mention the keyword once in the picture "Alt text" (see picture below).

The Alt text explains to blind readers what the picture is about - and - also to the Google bots who cannot read pictures, but need to be told what's in them. A great way to place your keywords...

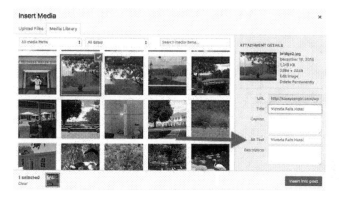

You can also change the picture url to your keyword before you upload into WP. Example in this case:

Victoria-Falls-Hotel.jpeg

With several pictures, mix it up. Don't use the keyword for every one to avoid over-optimizing/ keyword stuffing.

Rather use related or secondary keywords - or synonyms.

Video

Embed a video with the main keyword in the title. If you have your own, great - otherwise, search a relevant video on Youtube an embed within the article.

To embed a video into a post, simply copy and paste the Youtube url into the post text (within the "visual" WP editor), and the video will come up automatically.

Links

Have a least 1 outgoing link to an authority site, e.g. a wikipedia page covering your keyword topic, or any other well respected authoritative site.

This creates trustworthiness for the Google bots.

You don't need to mention Wikipedia or explain the link. Just place it on the keyword within your text, ideally more in the beginning. Remember, this is for SEO purposes, to create trustworthiness with the Google bots - not for your readers.

This is how you set up outgoing links:

Interlink

Always interlink with several other posts or pages on your blog. Something related, not just random.

Use "Link to existing content" to connect internally.

A little trick for both outgoing and interlinking:

Click "Open link in a new Tab". That way the initial page stays open while the reader is looking at the new page => counts towards the time visitors spend on your site => decreases bounce rate.... (see Chapter 3)

Meta Description

The meta description is the text people see when your page shows up in the SERPs. Another important area to mention your keyword once - but NO more than that. You can also use an alternate keyword with the same meaning (LSI).

To edit your meta data, scroll down from your post editor all the way to *Yoast SEO*. You will see this box:

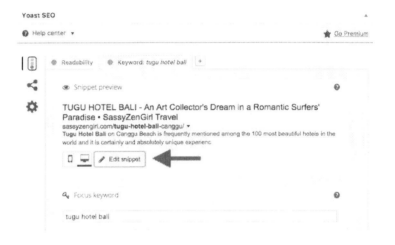

Click "Edit snippet" and adjust the text. The editor will show you how long your text can be, e.g. how much will be visible in the SERPs.

You can also edit your social media snippets here, if you want them to be different:

Yoast SEO Plugin

Scroll down a little further and you will see this box:

First you need to enter your target keyword, right under the snippet editor, and then Yoast will show you how well optimized your post is.

Ideally, all will be green. Otherwise, correct anything that's orange or red.

Occasionally, that won't be possible or sensible - and that's ok. You will know best.

It's simply automated feedback from a plugin - not Google itself - and for the most part very accurate.

Word Count

Overall, your posts should have a minimum of 500 words to appear relevant in Google's eyes. Even that number is pretty low. 1000 is where it really starts for SEO purposes. Google loves long, in-depth content and won't even consider anything below a certain word count.

Indexing your Posts

For SEO purposes it is important to get your posts and pages indexed as soon as possible. "Indexed" means, the Google bots have crawled and catalogued the page, and it's showing it in the search results.

An easy way to let Google know about new pages - or updates to existing pages - is a free service called **Pingomatic**.

It will automatically "ping" your post as soon as you click "update", and is an easy way to speed up the indexing process.

First go to *pingomatic.com* and enter your site. Then go to your WP Admin board and paste:

https://pingomatic.com

into the "*Update Services*" box under *Settings -> Writing*:

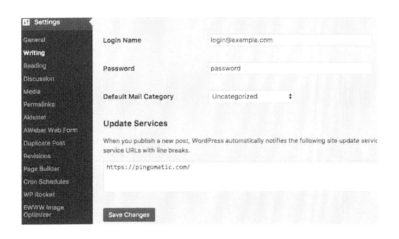

To check whether a page has been indexed, enter the following into the Google search bar:

Site:YourUrl.com

(Obviously replace "yoururl.com" with your specific post url).

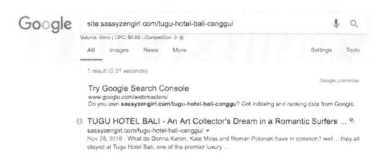

Chapter 3 - Off Page SEO

What is Off Page SEO?

Off Page SEO describes all external factors that influence how Google views your site. These can be grouped into 3 main categories:

* Traffic = number and length of visits to your site

* Social Signals

* Backlinks

Lets look at each individually:

Traffic

Google watches how many visitors you have per day - and - just as important - how long they stay. If you get 10,000 daily visitors and they all leave within 10 seconds, Google will interpret this as low quality. This is called "Bounce Rate".

In the above case, if people found you through a Google search, Google will assume that your site is not relevant to the search term people entered, and your ranking will drop.

Your *Google Analytics* account will give you a good idea of your traffic stats and also where your traffic is coming from.

Social Signals

Social Media are Google's biggest competition, so they always watch what's happening and trending there.

If your posts get a lot of likes, shares and comments - in other words, a lot of interaction and feedback from your readers - it sends a strong signal to the Google bots, that your content is relevant and important.

Without any social media interaction, ranking will be very difficult and it also looks a little fishy since popular and relevant content is always shared on social media.

Be sure to have a Social Media share bar, ideally a floating one, that stays with the text while the reader scrolls down. A good, free option is *SumoMe* which you can download from within your WP Admin ares.

To help with social media interaction, invite readers to share your content at the end of each post or ask a question. More on Social Media Marketing in the next book of the series.

The *Click-to-Tweet* plugin is another great tool to encourage social sharing. In that case you use a quote from your post and make it available within your text to be tweeted by the reader, thereby giving you additional tweets and retweets.

Tweetable quotes are a simple and elegant way to bring more traffic from Twitter http://ctt.ec/n6oH1+ @nickchurick

⟶ CLICK TO TWEET

Backlinks
Backlinks are the currency of the internet. Links control ranking, so this is the most important area to apply.

Once again though - none of the above will have much effect if the On Page Optimization isn't done first. It all ties in together.

Make it a habit to apply the points from Chapter 2 with every single article you write from now on, so you are consistently sending signals to Google about:

1) what your site/article is about
2) that your site/article is relevant and authoritative
3) has a lot of Social Media and Comment interaction

What is a Backlink?

A backlink is a link from an outside source pointing to your site.

Here are the most common backlink sources:

* Other Websites
* Social Media, incl. *Youtube*
* Directory listings
* Press releases
* Forums & Bookmarking sites

These are the two parameters Google will look at with each backlink:

* Relevance
* Power

Relevance:

Lets say you have a dog sitting site, then dog or pet related sites would be considered relevant. A law office linking to your dog sitting site would not be relevant. The link can still carry some juice, but by far not as much as when the topics are related.

Power:

Refers to Domain authority (DA) and Trust Flow (TF) which we covered in the **Keyword chapter**. The higher the DA and TF of the sites that are linking to you = "Referring Domains", the more powerful the link.

As a rough guide - anything over 15 DA or TF is a decent backlink - higher than 30 or 40: very powerful.

Only few sites get past 50 or close to 100 and those are usually well known authority sites like the *New York Times, Apple, Harvard* or the *Huffington Post*.

Another group of high authority links are:

- .gov
- .edu

These extensions are highly regulated and therefore add a lot of trust to your site - from the Google bots' perspective (=signals).

If you know someone who works at a .gov or .edu and can get you a backlink from their site, don't hesitate to ask them.

Once again, Google wants to see whether your site is: relevant, trustworthy and important.

The more you can convince the Google bots that you are the best choice for all three, the higher you will rank - and that's really what SEO is all about.

There are numerous techniques to send that message to Google - some more legal than others - and a good SEO will know which ones to use - and when and how much.

Black Hat SEO for example, is pretty much about *simulating* powerful signals to the Google bots, e.g. artificially creating powerful backlinks through various techniques, thereby raising the stature of a site or specific article.

A common practice is to rent or buy powerful backlinks.

All this has to look completely natural to not raise any red flags - and the Google bots in turn are constantly on the lookout for anything fishy.

Unless you intend to become an expert SEO - and even then there is still a degree of risk - focus on the techniques taught in this book - or hire a trustworthy SEO to speed things up (not cheap though....).

Keyword research will be your greatest friend - and consistent effort!

You can still rank if you give it some time and don't run the risk of having your site banned.

We'll go over a number of perfectly legal, and very effective methods to get the ball rolling, so not to worry....

Best of all, you don't have to do it yourself, but can outsource most of this to other people and I will share a few of the *Fiverr* and *Konker* gigs I use so you have a place to start.

A word of Caution:
With SEO, be <u>very</u> careful whatever gigs you otherwise buy. They all promise the world, but unless you understand *exactly* what they are doing and what the risks are, don't let anyone touch your site!

Another quick note in this regard: initially, as you start building links, your ranking might actually go down or erratically jump up and down for a few weeks.

This is called a "Google Dance" and another feature of Google's new algorithm. The purpose once again is to weed out phonies and unethical, spammy sites who might panic and respond with even more aggressive tactics.

So remain unfazed, let it play out and wait 2-3 weeks. It will usually calm down and settle around a certain rank.

With everything we know, Google is still very much unpredictable and frequently changes its behavior. So the best strategy as a beginner is to keep it simple, apply what you learn here on a consistent basis, give it time and then celebrate when you see yourself at #1 for the first time.

It's an awesome moment!

….and with the right choice of Long Tail keywords not impossible at all….

Backlinking Techniques

6 Simple Ways to generate Backlinks:

* Social Media Profiles
This is the very first thing you should do after you built your new site!

Set up several social media profiles with your Blog /"Brand" Name. Be sure to interlink the profiles, meaning mention your other profiles in a post or tweet, or place clickable links in your "About" section wherever that is possible (Facebook for example).

Example for Facebook post:
"Hey guys - just letting you know about my knew Twitter page at (place the Twitter link)"

Once again, this is about establishing trust. A solidly interlinked net of social media profiles sends an important signal to Google that you are a real, legitimate business or entity.

When you are brand new, they don't know you. They don't know what your intentions are. If you just want to spam people and make a quick buck or are out to spread good, relevant information.

By setting up social profiles across the board - Facebook, Twitter, Google+, Linkedin, Instagram, Pinterest etc - you are spreading your brand. You are showing that you are the real deal - and you do what most new businesses would do to let the world know they exist....

* Directories & Associations

Similar concept - again establishing trust and legitimacy. Directories can include anything from Yelp to Yellow Pages, especially if you have a local audience or directories related to your field.

The more the better and be sure to always include the *exact* same information, e.g. exact same spelling of your brand name, address (if you include a business address), website url etc.

If you are looking to rank locally - or show in the maps - then you need to also list yourself on **GoogleMyBusiness**:

Google.com/business/

Same goes for Associations in your field. The more well known and established, the better, and, of course, you need to be able to place a clickable link to your website in any profile.

Clickable means when you click on it, you get sent to another page - links are usually blue and underlined. Sometimes you need to add http:// in front of your url to make it clickable - on Youtube for example.

This is the gig I use when starting a new site:

SassyZenGirl.com/Citations-Gig

This guy is a pro, 100% reliable and he does all the work for you. You get listed on 200+ Directories (= "Citations") and that is another thing you should do soon after building your site and setting up your social media profiles.

* **Press Releases**
Same idea as above. Press release links usually stay only for a few months, but can give you a nice initial boost of link juice - and help you get noticed by Google.

This is a gig I occasionally use:

SassyZenGirl.com/PR-Gig

* Guest Blogging

I talk about Guest Blogging at length in the **2nd book of this series**. It is one of the most important strategies to grow your blog audience by leveraging someone else's readership.

It is also a great way to build valuable backlinks!

Of course, you need to research DA and TF for any blog you consider for guest posts and if the numbers are high, a powerful backlink will be a nice by-product of your guest blogging efforts.

That is - *if* - the link is "Do Follow"! - Always ask the blogger and if isn't, you are wasting your time.

Whoever sets up the link can decide whether the link is "Do Follow" or "No Follow", the latter meaning that no link juice is passed on.

Guest blogs *should* always be "Do Follow", but you need to make sure.

The fastest way I found to get guest blogging gigs is **this course by Jon Morrow**, one of the top bloggers in the business.

SassyZenGirl.com/Guest-Blogging

It teaches you how to write, research trending topics and most of all how to approach and pitch to the top blogs in your industry. Best of all, it comes with a Little Black Book of editor emails for 100+ top blogs in all major niches.

I rarely recommend courses or spending money, but this is one of the few exceptions. It will jump start your blogging career as only few other methods can. So take a look.

* Forums & Blog Comments
Whenever you comment in a forum or leave a comment under a blog post, you can usually add your website.

This, too, creates a backlink to your site. While this link type is not very powerful, it still adds legitimacy - if the forums or blogs are in your niche (=relevance) and have high metrics (=authority).

Be sure though to leave only relevant comments that add value or ask a question. NEVER leave your website or an affiliate offer in the comment text. Otherwise, the blog owner might mark you as spam, and that's, of course, *not* the signal you want to send to google.

On that note - watch carefully who leaves comments underneath *your* posts. If they are spam and you don't delete them, it will reflect badly on your site (spammy outgoing links...)

Be sure to install a plugin called ***Akismet*** to filter out spammy comments (and there will be a lot....). That will sideline the majority before they ever get posted.

* Donation Links

Obviously, treat this one ethically, but here is goes:

Charities and other non-profits (cultural organizations for example) will often list donors on their website, and quite frequently you can include a backlink to your site.

These can be very powerful, depending on the organization. Sites like *The Red Cross* or *New York*

Philharmonic have very high metrics, so can be good backlinks.

Often, a minimum of just a $1 is enough to get listed, but I would recommend to be ethical and make a decent donation for a cause you really care about, rather than just racking up high power backlinks.

Up to you, of course.

If possible, try to stay within your genre as relevance is once again important to Google. But even if occasionally there is no connection, this will still get some link juice flowing your way.

* Ask for Links
Make a list of everyone you know and see if they have a website or work somewhere that does.

Then see, if some of those sites might be relevant to your niche, check their metrics (DA and TF as shown in the last chapter) and if they are at least 10-15 ask them for a link.

Most of the time, they won't know what you are talking about, which is great. Just tell them that you are learning the basics of SEO and what it takes to rank in Google and that backlinks are one of the most important factors. Offer to explain it to them as well, so they, too, can improve their ranking and more often than not, they will be happy to arrange it.

Even if you have friends with new sites, exchange links. Over time, those sites will grow in authority and every little bit helps.

I already mentioned .gov and .edu sites. If you know someone connected with either, ask them, too.

Before you start any link building, be sure to read the chapters about **anchor text** and **penalties** (often triggered by one-sided anchor text ratios....)

It is not complicated, but very important to do right from the start to not get yourself in trouble later on.

Anchor Text

What is Anchor Text?

"Anchor" refers to the link text. In other words, the text that is on the link.

It's very important to keep anchor text varied to avoid a penalty.

If you use the main keyword as your anchor text on most backlinks, you are likely to incur a penalty as it looks unnatural and would be considered an attempt to manipulate the algorithm for better ranking (another form of keyword stuffing).

It is therefore a subtle dance between a sufficient number of "Target" anchors (=anchors using the exact keyword) and other types of Anchor text.

Anchor Text Types

Lets use the keyword *Dog Training* as an example for a fictional site called *DoggyHeavenDogTraining.com*

Target Anchor

As described above, a target anchor uses the exact keyword = exact match,

Dog Training

Or uses the exact keyword in a phrase = phrase match

Best Labrador Dog Training

LSI Anchor

Uses a synonym to the main keyword

Canine Obedience Class

Brand Anchor

Uses your brand name = your name or your company/ blog name

Doggy Heaven

Naked url Anchor

http://doggyheavendogtraining.com

or

doggyheavendogtraining.com

Generic Anchor

"Click here" - *"more info here"* and similar

Misc. Anchor

unrelated words within the text as anchor

There is no one-fits-all solution, and anchor text ratios vary by niche - for now, just keep them mixed.

For important backlinks (from authority sites) use target anchors and LSIs.

For press releases and citation gigs ONLY use branded or naked url anchor (never the target keyword). In this way, those two gigs can also be used to spread anchor text ratio if you ever get over-optimized with too much target anchor.

Whenever you outsource link building (citation gigs, backlinking etc.), you will be asked to provide a list of anchors.

That's what the above is referring to.

To give you a visual reference, this is an Anchor Text pie chart - which shows the different anchor text types (=different colors) nicely spread out, instead of one having the majority of the pie.

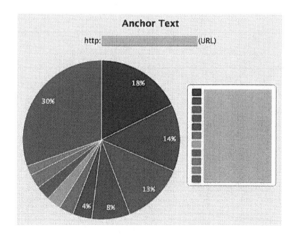

Most of all, in the beginning - don't stress too much it! No one will penalize you with a brand new site. Just be aware of the rules and use different anchors throughout your link building - and you will be fine.

By the time your site grows and starts ranking on page 1, you will be much more experienced and will know how to correct from there, if needed.

Google Penalties

I will briefly cover the current penalties and how to avoid them. If you apply what is taught here, it is very unlikely that you will ever have an issue, so don't worry too much, but it's important to at least know what they are about.

First of all, there are two different types of penalties: algorithmic and manual.

Algorithmic is triggered automatically when the Google bots crawl your site.

Manual means a human employee at Google has reviewed your site (usually triggered by an alert from the Google bots) and found it in violation of their policies.

Manual reviews will show in your *Google Search Console* under "Manual Review", so if ever you can't find your site - not even when entering site:yoururl.com - this is where you should look next.

Manual penalties are not as frequent and easier to fix, but either way you want to avoid penalties at all costs.

The two main algorithm updates in recent years were: **Panda** and **Penguin**.

Panda

Panda's 1st version came around in 2011 and focused mainly on **On Page** factors, in particular low quality content. This can be:

* very short content

* **spun content** - yes, there are actually softwares who spin an existing text to be reused on another site.

* Overall low quality: lots of spelling mistakes, grammatical errors, cookie-cutter or copied **("duplicate") content** without any new impulses

* Over-optimization: in particular, **keyword stuffing**

Once you are hit with a Panda penalty, it will apply to your entire site, not just the page that triggered it.

Penguin

Penguin's 1st version was launched in 2012 and focused mainly on **Off Page** factors, in particular your site's **link profile**.

Sites with unnatural or a large number of spammy links were penalized or at least dropped in the rankings.

Very importantly, anchor text ratio became an important ranking factor. More on **anchor text ratio** in the previous chapter.

One major recent update included Penguin 4.0 which made the Penguin algorithm 24/7. Meaning it is now running constantly and not just once or twice a year - which is good news!

Yes, it is easier now to get caught, but it is also much easier - and faster - to get an algorithmic penalty removed.

In the past, when you were hit with a penalty, you made corrections and adjustments and then had to wait until Penguin was run again, which could be many months. Now when you make the proper adjustments and corrections, you can get your ranking back right away. So much better.

Other penalties include:

* **Mobile Friendly** - websites now have to be mobile compatible and be fully functional on mobile devices

* **Top Heavy** - a site that's so overloaded with ads that visitors have a hard time finding the actual content

* **Payday** - dubious payday loan sites and similar

* **Pirate** - sites that offer pirated content

How to recover from a Penalty?

Hopefully, you will never have to ask that question, but if you ever do, this article goes in-depth on how to recover from a penalty and get your ranking back.

SassyZenGirl.com/Google-Recovery

Want to know more...?

Well....there you have it...;-)

An overview over what SEO stands for, how it works, and the main techniques to help you get started and increase your authority and trustworthiness with Google.

SEO is a complex, ever changing science, but some principles remain steady, and we covered them all in this book.

I strongly recommend that you stay at least peripherally updated on Google's algorithm changes and SEO updates.

One of the best sites to help you with that - and a source of many more in-depth articles - is:

BackLinko.com

Brian Dean has become one of the top authorities in SEO, and White Hat SEO in particular. Subscribe to his newsletter and be sure to read whenever he has a new article (or video).

They are all well written and easy to understand and will keep you abreast of anything you need to know - and occasionally show you more in-depth techniques and tips.

For more traffic generation techniques, be sure to check out the other books in this series:

#1 How to Start a Blog (technical set up)

#2 How to Grow an Audience:
incl. researching trending topics, the writing style of blogging and how to monetize your blog

#4 Social Media Marketing

#5 Kindle Publishing - Write a Bestseller in 30 Days!
one of *the* most effective traffic generation machines (on autopilot) and a great way to build authority in your niche and with your readers.

I wish you all the very best &
Happy Blogging,

Gundi Gabrielle
SassyZenGirl.com/Freedom

More SassyZenGirl Yummies

COURSES

SassyZenGirl's Blogging Bootcamp
SassyBlogBootcamp.com

FREE Masterclass:
POWER MARKETING BLUEPRINT
DreamClientsOnAutopilot.com

Award Winning
INFLUENCER FAST TRACK
Series

#1 Bestselling
BEGINNER INTERNET MARKETING
Series
"The Sassy Way... when you have NO CLUE!"

#1 *Bestselling*
TRAVEL BOOKS

Score FREE Flights, Rental
Cars & Accommodations.
Dramatically reduce Airfares.
Get paid to Travel & START a
DIGITAL NOMAD BIZ
you can run from anywhere
in the world!

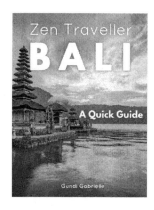

**ZEN TRAVELLER
BALI**
A QUICK GUIDE

Explore the "real" Bali…
The quiet, magical parts
far away from the
tourist crowds…

About the Author

Gundi Gabrielle, aka *SassyZenGirl*, loves to explain complex matters in an easy to understand, fun way. Her *"The Sassy Way...when you have NO CLUE!!"* series has helped thousands around the world conquer the jungles of internet marketing with humor, simplicity and some sass.

A 11-time #1 Bestselling Author, Entrepreneur and former Carnegie Hall conductor, Gundi employs marketing chops from all walks of life and loves to help her readers achieve their dreams in a practical, fun way. Her students have published multiple #1 Bestsellers outranking the likes of Tim Ferris, John Grisham, Hal Elrod and Liz Gilbert.

When she is not writing books or enjoying a cat on her lap (or both), she is passionate about exploring the world as a Digital Nomad, one awesome adventure at a time.

She has no plans of settling down anytime soon.

SassyZenGirl.com
SassyZenGirl.Group
DreamClientsOnAutopilot.com

Instagram.com/SassyZenGirl
Youtube.com/c/SassyZenGirl
Facebook.com/SassyZenGirl
Twitter.com/SassyZenGirl